Original title:
Feathers on the Horizon

Copyright © 2025 Creative Arts Management OÜ
All rights reserved.

Author: Levi Montgomery
ISBN HARDBACK: 978-1-80586-129-4
ISBN PAPERBACK: 978-1-80586-601-5

Wings Crafted in Stardust

A chicken dreams of flying high,
With wings adorned in cosmic spry.
She struts about in feathered pride,
While hiding from the cat outside.

A pigeon's on a cosmic spree,
Collecting stars for tea and glee.
He wears a hat, it's quite the sight,
And dances like a disco knight.

Sails of the Morning Mist

A seagull sails on coffee steam,
While sharing gossip, oh so cream!
With whispers sweet and crumbs galore,
He claims the skies, but checks the floor.

The sparrows plan a grand parade,
With tiny flags, they're unafraid.
Their tunes are set, with beats and claps,
They flutter by like chirpy chaps.

The Boundless Veil of Blue

A duck in shades, quite cool, you see,
Sings pop songs to the bumblebee.
With sunglasses on, he struts the shore,
Claiming he's a rockstar, nothing more.

The robins join with rhythm tight,
Playing hopscotch, oh what a sight!
They leap and twirl with silly grace,
As clouds compete in a puffy race.

Whispers of a Gentle Breeze

A parrot chats with quite the flair,
Confessing secrets in the air.
He tells of tales from high above,
Of peanut butter and sweet love.

A raven swoops in like a boss,
Boasting stories, oh what a loss!
With every caw, he leaves us laughing,
In a world of whimsy, ever crafting.

A Journey Through Feathered Dreams

In a land where pillows float,
Chickens dance with coats of goat.
Ducks wear hats, oh what a sight,
Silly birds take to the night.

One parrot tells a joke so sweet,
While flamingos do the cha-cha beat.
Pigeons in tuxedos wink and stride,
As laughter echoes far and wide.

Light's Dance Above the World

A swan in stilettos prances high,
While sparrows practice their lullaby.
Silly geese in bow ties roam,
Each twist and flap feels like home.

The sun throws sparkles, a dazzling show,
As birds all flaunt their fashion glow.
Kites made of paper soar and dive,
In this carnival, we're all alive!

Transient Echoes of Flight

A parakeet wears shades of green,
With a feathered friend, a clownish scene.
Flip-flops on the peacock's feet,
He struts around, oh what a feat!

The owls hoot with giggles bright,
Trading jokes beneath the moonlight.
Quirky ravens sing with flair,
In this realm of the odd and rare.

Where Wishes Take Wing

A pelican with popcorn dreams,
Dances with a flock of themes.
With tiny wings, they take their flight,
Making wishes on stars at night.

Hummingbirds sip on lemonade,
While butterflies play charades in shade.
Here, every giggle helps you soar,
In this world where fun's in store!

Whispers of the Skies

Silly birds chatter, thinking they're wise,
Telling tall tales about all the flies.
They flip and they flop with such grand designs,
Who knew a pigeon could stand in such lines?

Clouds wear their shades, gossiping high,
While rainbows play tricks, oh my, oh my!
Each giggle a gust that tickles the trees,
Nature's own joke, carried on a breeze.

Dreams Take Flight

A chicken in sneakers, sprinting for fun,
Chasing its dreams, thinking it's number one.
While ducks in bowties swim straight to the bank,
Counting their coins with a quack and a prank.

The eagle's got jokes, a comedian's flair,
Telling the hawk that it's losing its hair.
With laughter like wind that swirls all around,
It's a comedy show high up from the ground.

Plumes Against the Sunset

In a world painted orange, a parrot takes aim,
Squawking out truths like it's winning a game.
As twilight descends, the owls hoot in glee,
Making wisecracks as funny as can be.

Gliding through colors that dazzle the eye,
The starlings take selfies, oh my, oh my!
With filters of clouds and a sparkle of light,
They post and they laugh till it's way past night.

Wings of Distant Dreams

A flamingo in slippers, prancing on sand,
Twirling and whirling, oh isn't it grand?
While seagulls compete in a dive for a fry,
Who needs fancy dinners when food's on the fly?

Cloud puff comedians, dancing so spry,
Tickle the herons, oh woe to the shy!
With chuckles in feathers, they soar through the air,
Creating a spectacle, silly and rare.

Glimmers in the Twilight Sky

Stars peek out with a cheeky grin,
Dancing around like they're all in kin.
A comet trips, spills stardust bright,
And giggles echo in the velvet night.

Moonbeams waltz with cloudy fluff,
While whispers of dreams say, "That's enough!"
A firefly blinks, mischief in each glow,
It's a cosmic party, putting on quite a show.

Twirling with the Breeze

Breezes giggle, swirling around,
Tickling the grass without a sound.
Kites are screaming, go higher, go fast,
As squirrels join in with a happy blast.

Dandelions laugh, they're on the run,
"Catch us if you can," they shout in fun.
A butterfly sneezes, sends petals on flights,
Dance, dear nature, into the nights.

Traces of Luminous Wanders

A wandering star trips over a cloud,
And chuckles softly, feeling quite proud.
Moonlight splashes, slips into trees,
Painting the world with giggly degrees.

Comets munch on cosmic pies,
Jupiter laughs, "Cut me a slice!"
While Saturn spins rings, making them bright,
Creating a ruckus in the quiet night.

A Flight of Imagination

What if clouds wore shoes, oh my delight!
They'd prance and dance, a whimsical sight.
Imagine the raindrops on pogo sticks,
Bouncing around with their splashy tricks.

If wishes had wings, they'd zoom and glide,
Chasing the sun, what a rollercoaster ride!
A parade of dreams would march in line,
Singing and laughing, oh, how divine!

Ascending into Tranquility

A chicken flew up high, oh dear,
Clucking loudly, spreading cheer.
In a tutu and a crown, it spun,
Who said farm life couldn't be fun?

The cows looked up, their eyes wide,
As the chicken danced with pride.
Beefy pals had jokes to share,
Why's that chicken up in the air?

A goat joined in with a bleat so bold,
Wishing for wings, or so we're told.
They formed a troupe in the sunny glade,
Belly laughs with every charade.

Now every dawn, from barn to sky,
They're the stars of a circus, oh my!
With a wink and a flap, they take their flight,
In the heart of the farm, humor takes height.

Skylit Ascension

A pigeon once tried to be a star,
Wore sunglasses and went too far.
When it landed, it slipped on a pie,
And left the world asking, 'Oh why?'

The seagulls cackled, 'What a sight!'
As it waddled back, feeling light.
With a song and a quack, they formed a band,
The best comedy troupe in the land.

They flew on kites through the cloudy bliss,
Singing tunes that you couldn't miss.
With a waddle and a flap, they danced in pairs,
A feast of giggles, laughter in airs.

So next time you watch, take a glance,
At birds in hats, they're in a dance.
Just something to lighten the day,
As birds do tricks, hip-hip-hooray!

Dreams Adrift in Ether

In a dream, a duck wore shades,
Floating through an escapade.
It quacked a song about the moon,
While sipping tea, it hummed a tune.

A fish swam high, a sight indeed,
With bubble jokes, it took the lead.
Giggling clouds gathered 'round to see,
"That's the silliest fish, oh agree!"

A squirrel cheese-surfed on a star,
Spreading laughter from near to far.
With every tumbling, splashing cheer,
He brought the cosmos close and near.

So when you snooze and dreams ignite,
Look for wonders in the night.
Because laughter flies on the softest breeze,
Just like playful whispers through the trees.

The Weight of a Feather's Touch

A wise old owl sat on a perch,
With tales of cats and an old church.
He chuckled loud, 'They think they're slick,'
But feathery fables will do the trick.

Sparrows played pranks on the neighbor's cat,
Swapping its hat with a lovely mat.
While the cat just stared, all around,
'Is this feather? I'll wear it proud!'

From tree to tree, the gossip flew,
'Have you heard? A raccoon tried to skate too!'
Can't balance life on a tippy toe,
With fluffy fluff, the giggles flow.

In the end, it's a feather's grace,
That turns our frowns to a silly face.
So let's all laugh at the silly side,
For humor takes flight, far and wide.

Skyward Reveries

Birds in pajamas, dancing in flight,
Chasing the sun, from morning to night.
Worms throw a party, in tree trunks they hide,
While squirrels play tag, on a tree branch slide.

Clouds wear the silliest hats, oh my!
A top hat, a beret, floating on high.
A raccoon in shades sips lemonade sweet,
As the skies giggle, twirling on their feet.

Kites get jealous, pulling at strings,
While butterflies argue about colorful things.
With laughter and jests, the air fills with cheer,
As the sun winks down, "Let's party, my dear!"

The horizon's a canvas, splashed with bright hues,
As starfish wear sneakers and puff up balloon moos.
Together they frolic, in realms up above,
Creating a circus, that sings of our love.

The Untamed Arc of Morning

Ducks don their swimwear, splashing about,
While roosters throw parties, making a clout.
The world wakes in giggles, with sleepy-eyed glee,
As toast bites the butter, like it's a spree.

Jellybeans tumble from clouds overhead,
As pancakes twirl round like they've just been fed.
The coffee pot winks, more jittery than beans,
While toast takes a bow, in buttery sheens.

Bees perform ballet, in flowers of fun,
Each petal a stage, in the warmth of the sun.
Life's a grand circus, a whimsical show,
With laughter as fuel, let our joy overflow!

The morning sky chuckles, tickling our faces,
With buttered croissants and syrupy laces.
So let's dive together into this delight,
As dawn paints the world, all merry and bright.

A Symphony Written in Light

A symphony stirs where the skylarks play,
With drum rolls of thunder at the break of day.
Dancing with shadows, each note takes a flight,
While sunlight composes a marvellous sight.

The whispers of breezes sing melodies sweet,
As sunshine tiptoes on little birds' feet.
Rainbows glance sideways, a cheeky tableau,
Playing peek-a-boo with the world down below.

The sun's playful laughter, a melody bright,
Acknowledges mischief in the broad daylight.
As the grass giggles and the daisies sway,
Together they croon in a whimsical way.

So grab your umbrella for the sprinkles of cheer,
As songs in the air spread each giggle near.
With each note a smile, let the laughter take flight,
In a symphony spun from the warm morning light.

Beneath the Gaze of the Sky

Under the gaze of clouds fluffing their tails,
Critters devise their amusing trails.
The cat wears a crown, the dog dons a cape,
While ants hold a conference on how to escape.

A snail brings a snack to the birds in debate,
As butterflies gossip, wearing shades of fate.
The fish jiggle smiles from ponds down below,
While turtles shake hands to solidify flow.

Frisbees are soaring on invisible streams,
As sunlight casts shadows with the weirdest dreams.
Every critter gathers, the sky holds the cheer,
Sipping on clouds, oh so offered at dear.

Beneath this vast canvas of whimsy and jest,
Where laughter is woven, making hearts feel blessed.
With mirth as our guide, we skip through the day,
As the sky chuckles softly, "Come out and play!"

The Whispering Skies

Up above, the clouds conspire,
To talk about a silly choir.
Balloons float by, wearing hats,
Dancing with the chatting rats.

A pigeon plots a joyful prank,
While squirrels giggle on a plank.
Each giggle makes the sunbeam blush,
As zephyrs swirl in merry hush.

With every breeze, the tales unfold,
Of cheeky crows and daring bold.
They cackle jokes that tickle ears,
In skies where laughter conquers fears.

So gaze up high, let spirits lift,
Embrace the skies, a joyful gift.
For nature's jesters take their flight,
In clouds of whimsy, pure delight.

Glances at the Infinite

Above the trees, a wink so sly,
As kites attempt to touch the sky.
A lofty breeze gives whispers low,
While stars in jest begin to glow.

A squirrel, dressed in dapper ties,
Rehearses jokes to passing flies.
He flips a nut with perfect flair,
While giggling moonbeams tease the air.

Each glimmer holds a secret grin,
As shadows prance, letting fun begin.
The constellations chuckle soft,
As they dance 'round, and lift aloft.

So take a peek, what will you find?
A comic world, hilariously blind.
In laughter's light, we'll take our chance,
As stars prepare for an endless dance.

Twilight's Mythos

When dusk descends, the jokes ignite,
With owls that hoot in sheer delight.
Fireflies twinkle like laughing stars,
As rabbits play their little guitars.

A raccoon juggles all his dreams,
With snacks that fall and burst their seams.
He bows and winks, the crowd's a buzz,
In nature's show, the biggest fuzz.

The moon complains of wearied beams,
As shadows spin their silly schemes.
Each gust of wind sends chuckles flying,
While colorful clouds are slyly spying.

So come and join this twilight fest,
Where myth and laughter intertwine best.
In every giggle, bright and bold,
Lies the magic that never gets old.

Nestled in the Zenith

Atop the hills, the breezes play,
With twinkling joy that skips away.
A dandy duck gives silly waves,
To all the clouds that float like braves.

Each tree leans in to share a jest,
Unruly leaves all look impressed.
A bluejay flaps his wings in mirth,
As laughter echoes round the earth.

Through giggles soft, the cosmos swirl,
As sunbeams dance and twirl and twirl.
The sky's a canvas, bright and bold,
Filled with wonders yet untold.

So look above, let spirits soar,
Find giggly magic and explore.
For in each laugh, a wish can fly,
As dreams take wing and drift on high.

A Feather's Last Farewell

A feather took a flight, oh so bold,
It whispered dreams of stories untold.
With every gust it danced, so carefree,
Until it tangled in a squirrel's spree.

It tried to wave goodbye with a twirl,
But ended up stuck in a postman's whirl.
With letters flying in every direction,
The feather sighed at its grand misdirection.

From tree to mailbox, a wild parade,
A pigeon laughed loud, 'What a charade!'
But through all the fuss, it laughed with glee,
For life's quite a laughter, just wait and see!

As the sun set low, the feather sighed,
It found new friends on this crazy ride.
With a wink to the wind, it felt so spry,
It whispered, "Next time, I'll just learn to fly!"

Veils of the Cosmic Wind

In a breeze of cosmic chuckles, they float,
A band of confetti, from the heavens, they gloat.
They giggle with clouds in a mission so bold,
To sprinkle some joy on the earth below.

A comet blinked twice at the shimmering sight,
'Hey, keep it down! I'm trying to write!'
But the feathers kept laughing, spinning in space,
Creating a ruckus, oh what a race!

A star joined the dance with a twinkling blink,
"It's hard to be serious with drinks that you sink!"
The laughter erupted through galaxies wide,
With each silly swish, their joy couldn't hide.

But soon they grew tired, and the giggles would cease,
As the cosmic wind lulled them into peace.
With a flutter and flap, they drifted in sway,
Promising mischief for another day.

The Forgotten Language of the Sky

In the morning light, a ruckus unfolds,
As birds chirp secrets that nobody holds.
A feathered diplomat joins the debate,
"Let's solve this puzzle before it's too late!"

With beaks all a-flutter, they speak in a spin,
Oh, what a confusion, where do I begin?
A parrot squawks loudly, claiming the crown,
While a finch flutters 'round, dragging it down.

They hold a convention up high in the trees,
Swapping old stories and making up tease.
A duck quacks a punchline; the crowd goes aloof,
"Was that a real joke or just a bad hoof?"

Yet under the chaos, a lesson appears,
That laughter and friendship can conquer all fears.
So if you listen closely, you'll hear the reply:
In the dance of the breeze, we are all spry.

Surreal Sojourns Above

A chicken in a bowler hat,
Danced with clouds that wore a cat.
They twirled through skies, a comical sight,
While pastries rained down, oh what a flight!

The sun wore shades, a sunny grin,
While stars cracked jokes, oh where to begin?
A cow jumped high, then lost its place,
And landed right in a toaster's embrace!

Birds sang songs of silly tales,
Of diving through rivers filled with snails.
A merry-go-round of joyous refrain,
As fruitcake raindrops danced in the lane!

With laughter echoing, time took a chance,
To waltz along in a whimsical dance.
The breeze was chuckling, oh what a treat,
In this odd world, where joy and humor meet!

Harmonies of the Ethereal

A jester with wings began to glide,
Over trees where veggies hide.
He strummed a lute made of spaghetti,
While noodles bounced like jelly confetti!

The moon wore a tutu, bright and round,
As squirrels played drums on the ground.
Peanuts and popcorn formed a band,
Chirping and chirping, oh so grand!

With telephones dressed as hats galore,
They called on the clouds for encore.
Twisting and twirling on dreamlike lanes,
With giggles that echoed like joyous refrains!

Traffic signs giggled, lost their way,
As traffic lights threw a bright cabaret.
In the park where laughter is free,
Silly songs sang, quite joyfully!

Gliding through Celestial Realms

A llama wore wings, took to the sky,
Spinning in circles, oh me, oh my!
He whispered secrets to the cool breeze,
As jellybeans danced among the trees!

Balloons with faces floated past,
Tickling the sun, oh what a blast!
They wrapped around stars just for fun,
Crafting a constellation, one by one!

A parade of turtles laughed and cheered,
While toasted marshmallows appeared.
With sprinkles sparkling like fairy dust,
They pranced along; in fun, we trust!

And as the night began to unfold,
Stories of laughter and love were told.
In realms where giggles sweetly bloom,
Silly dreams chased away the gloom!

The Poetry of Lightness

A whimsical breeze played the flute,
While daisies danced in a polka-dot suit.
They jived with the daffodils, quite absurd,
Singing sweet nothings without a word!

Up in the air, a duck did a flip,
Riding on rainbows, taking a trip.
With gumballs rolling atop cotton candy,
And sticky ice cream making laughs dandy!

Lollipops giggled, spinning with glee,
As jellyfish roamed the land of the free.
Frolicking softly above hill and dale,
On a train made of muffins, we set sail!

From sunrise to sunset, a perfect jest,
In this world where shenanigans rest.
So lift up your spirits, come join the fun,
With each silly moment, there's laughter for everyone!

Embrace of the Aerial Ballet

When birds take a leap and twirl,
They spin like a kite in a whirl.
With flapping and flailing, oh what a sight,
They dance through the air, full of delight.

The pigeons compete in a choreographed show,
While crows mock them with a swaggering flow.
A seagull swoops down, steals the lead,
"Hey, pass me a fry!"—it's a feathered creed.

With a flutter and flap, they each take a bow,
Trying to steal each other's' wow.
As winds pick up speed, catch them in flight,
They giggle and guffaw, oh what a sight!

So join in the laughter, just take to the sky,
Where the birds throw a party, oh my, oh my!
With each little joke in their flight so absurd,
Who knew that the skies could be so wordy?

The Language of Windswept Visions

The breeze carries gossip, oh so sweet,
As sparrows gossip, with a tweet.
They chirp about trends in the plumage race,
And fashion faux pas that happen in space.

The ducks quack in code, a riddle and rhyme,
While geese giggle loudly, causing a crime.
They flap their big wings, landing like stars,
Sharing tales of adventures in faraway bars.

A parrot pops in, with a bright outfit,
Telling silly stories that just won't quit.
The owls roll their eyes, their wisdom unmatched,
"Can't someone just hush? We've all been dispatched!"

But still, in this chaos, the laughter soars,
With each little quirk that nature adores.
A mix of intentions in this clamor of noise,
It's a beautiful mess as the sky becomes poise.

Crescendos of Color in Flight

In a world painted bright, all the colors collide,
As birds flaunt their feathers, like they're on a ride.
Every flap is a canvas, each squawk is a hue,
A circus of shades, oh what a view!

The blue jays argue, "I'm the brightest here!"
While cardinals chirp, "Oh, please, have no fear!"
The canaries add jokes, with a giggle and peep,
A tapestry woven from laughter so deep.

With a flash and a flap, they swoop and they soar,
Chasing each other to settle the score.
In this colorful ruckus, their spirits ignite,
With a dash of hilarity, they own the night.

So come join the frenzy, no time to be shy,
In the show of the feathered, just look to the sky.
Where each vivid glance, and each chuckle is free,
And the air fills with joy, like a symphony.

The Lure of Ethereal Adrift

Up in the clouds, a feathered crew plays,
With antics so wacky, they baffle and graze.
They're sailing the skies in an airborne parade,
In costumes of whimsy that never can fade.

A rubber chicken lands, just made quite the splash,
A flock of ducklings burst forth with a dash.
They waddle and wobble with laughter so loud,
Taking pride in the silliness, feeling so proud.

"Did you hear about Fred? He forgot how to fly!"
He honks at the joke and gives it a try.
Flapping and flailing, he spirals around,
Creating a spectacle while falling to ground.

With giggles and chirps, their laughter ignites,
They twirl through the air, adding spark to the nights.
So let go of worries, just float among dreams,
As the sky bursts with humor and whimsical themes.

Silken Tales of the Sky

A chicken dreams, it takes to flight,
With high hopes of swooping in the night.
But plucking clouds with floppy wings,
It finds that much flies, but laughter sings.

A duck in shades, with shades on beak,
Quacks out jokes that leave us weak.
The sky's a stage for every fowl,
As they prance about and sweetly prowl.

An owl tells tales of midnight cheer,
While pigeons plot their picnic here.
On warm winds their giggles drift,
In feathered gowns, their spirits lift.

With every flap and every quack,
The skies burst forth with laughter's knack.
Each feathered friend, a comic tale,
Painting smiles as they sail and sail.

The Gentle Brush of Morning Light

A rooster's crow, a jester's call,
It cracks us up as daylight falls.
With messy hair from dreaming flight,
He crows and struts, a morning rite.

The sun sneezes rays that tickle the grass,
As sparrows giggle, their antics pass.
They wear their shades, they're oh-so-cool,
Imitating the sun, just breaking rule.

A parrot rips a joke from thin air,
His punchline, squawked without a care.
With every squabble, every tease,
The dawn bursts forth, all spirits seize.

Bright laughter paints the skies anew,
On humor's brush, fresh scenes ensue.
With morning light as our trusty guide,
We spread our laughs, let joy abide!

Shadows of Grace Above

A finch in flight, quite out of kilter,
Trips on air, but still the filter!
With dips and dives, it makes a scene,
Like a ballet in a dream—so keen!

Clouds sip tea while watching below,
As geese parade, a fancy show.
In mismatched socks, they honk in glee,
Their ruffled tales, a sight to see!

A swan must tussle with wind's big hand,
Doubling over—oh, isn't life grand?
With shimmering grace, it slips with style,
Painting the air with each silly smile.

In shadows dancing, all creatures play,
And laughter sparkles like bright bouquet.
Their stories float on breeze-filled grace,
Billed with joy, it's a grand embrace.

A Palette of Airborne Hues

A parakeet in hues of blue,
Spills the paint in a joyous hue.
With splashes bright that whirl and twirl,
It crafts a storm with a fluttered swirl.

Canaries laugh in golden cheer,
As they paint the sky with little sneers.
They hold a brush, and oh so sly,
They tickle clouds, watch colors fly!

Roll out the scroll of dreams so wide,
Where humor glows, and spirits ride.
With strokes of jest, they color the sky,
A masterpiece that makes us sigh.

Each vibrant laugh, a joyful shade,
In the painting of life, no moment delayed.
Wings dipped in laughter, skies that amuse,
In the palette of joy, we joyfully fuse!

Clouded Pathways of Grace

I tripped on a cloud, collector of dreams,
With giggles and chuckles, it burst at the seams.
A squirrel in suspenders, a parrot with flair,
We danced through the giggles, lost in the air.

The sun wore a top hat, quite jolly, I swear,
It spun like a ballerina without any care.
A kite on a leash ran away with my shoe,
And owls played the lute, singing songs just for two.

The rain drops were jellybeans, sweet when they fell,
I twirled through the puddles, enchanting and swell.
With vaporous giggles, the sky gave a nod,
To the dance of the day, a humorous trod.

Then a crow stole my sandwich, cheeky, and bold,
As I chased through the clouds, laughter uncontrolled.
With every misstep, the world seemed to grin,
On clouded pathways, where funny dreams spin.

Soft Light Falling

A candle mainstay, soft flickers ignite,
As rabbits in tuxedos sneak into the light.
They jive with the shadows, a tap dance delight,
While owls in glasses assess the first sight.

The moon played a trick, tying stars in a bow,
And whispers of laughter echoed below.
A penguin in shades slid right down the hill,
With a wink and a twirl, oh, what a thrill!

The breeze carried giggles, a soft, gentle tease,
As dandelions danced, swaying with ease.
Chasing sunbeams, we lost track of time,
In this soft light falling, laughter was prime.

A turtle made jokes, slow but precise,
While squirrels debated, "Should we take some rice?"
With every odd moment, we chuckled and played,
In bright falling light, all the worries delayed.

The Elegy of Lost Wings

Once flew with the sparrows, with style and grace,
But slipped on a banana peel, fell from my place.
A crow now my rival, with tales quite absurd,
I'd pin my old hopes on a passing bird.

In dreams, I ascended, soared high above trees,
While llamas below swayed and giggled with ease.
My spirit now caught in a web of delight,
With the bees as my chorus, I took off in flight.

The clouds had a party, confetti and cheer,
And I pulled on my strings, no longer in fear.
The whispers of nonsense floated through the air,
In elegy spoken with laughter to share.

But time plays tricks, like a clown in disguise,
As balloons laughed at me, oh, what a surprise!
Lost wings turned to giggles, a dance of the heart,
In the realm of the silly, I played my part.

Flight Paths in Twilight

The twilight spun colors, like cotton candy skies,
As crickets donned suits, with mischievous eyes.
A frog hopped around with a crown made of leaves,
While fireflies twinkled like bright, laughing thieves.

A giraffe told a story, so tall it's a craze,
Of penguins while surfing on colorful waves.
The owls brought the snacks, a buffet on the rise,
As laughter erupted, oh, what a surprise!

With every soft whisper and secretive glance,
The twilight accepted our giggling dance.
A walrus played chess with a cat dressed in suits,
Find joy in the oddities, oh, life's just so cute!

As I soared through the twilight, full of delight,
In the flight paths of magic, I twirled through the night.
With every odd creature that danced in the glow,
The humor of twilight continued to flow.

Cascading Dreams Above

Fluffy clouds in silly dance,
They slip and slide, they take a chance.
A pogo stick, a laugh, a cheer,
Who knew dreams could leap so near?

A paper plane with a goofy grin,
Zooming past, it yells, "Let's win!"
A race with raindrops, come what may,
They giggle, tumble, splashing play.

Socks that twirl in the summer breeze,
Chasing giggles among the trees.
They'd rather skip than sit around,
With joyful leaps, they hit the ground!

In the distance, a rainbow snores,
Colorful snickers at the shores.
As dreams cascade like jelly beans,
They bounce and play in laughter's scenes.

Beyond the Amber Sky

Bees in bow ties, buzzing loud,
Throwing parties with a proud crowd.
Dancing daisies in the glow,
Sipping sunshine from below.

Puffball clouds in a bright parade,
Chasing each other, a charade.
Ticklish breezes whisper sweet,
While butterflies tap-dance on their feet.

A trampoline of laughter soars,
Bouncing dreams across the shores.
With every leap, they swirl and glide,
Making the universe their slide.

In this realm where quirks collide,
Silly antics, they cannot hide.
Beyond the amber, joy does fly,
As laughter echoes in the sky.

Starlit Moments in Motion

Twinkling stars wear goofy hats,
Dancing with the playful bats.
They spin on beams of shimmering light,
Creating giggles through the night.

Moonbeams surf on cosmic waves,
While comets tease, the night behaves.
Shooting stars that trip and fall,
Shouting, "Oops!" they laugh through all.

Galactic junk, a whimsical mess,
Doodles of dreams, no need to stress.
In silly orbits round they go,
These starlit moments steal the show!

So grab a sparkler, make a wish,
Join the party, it's quite delish!
In motion here, we'll dance and sway,
Underneath the stars that play.

Gentle Currents of Bliss

Waves that tickle sandy toes,
Giggling shells, where mischief flows.
A beach ball bounces, round and wide,
As sunbeams rocket down the tide.

Seagulls squawk in silly voice,
Making jokes, they rejoice.
Crab competes in a silly race,
As laughter echoes in this place.

Kites that flutter, tails in a spin,
Whipping up winds where fun begins.
In gentle currents, we ride the bliss,
Chasing joy with a playful kiss.

So come along to this funtime fest,
Where laughter lulls and dreams invest.
With every wave, let worries cease,
In these gentle currents, find your peace.

Soaring Beyond the Clouds

Up in the air, a chicken flew,
With dreams of heights and skies so blue.
It flapped and flailed, a silly sight,
Chasing sunbeams, oh what a flight!

Pigeons played tag, they thought it cool,
While ducks practiced lines in their own school.
They quacked with laughter, a raucous cheer,
As one gave a speech, the crowd drew near!

A seagull swooped down, trying to dance,
In a tuxedo, oh what a chance!
But tripped on its tail, went head over heels,
Landed in popcorn, what a meal!

So next time you gaze at the sprawling sky,
Remember the fowl that can really fly.
They may look silly, but they know what's true:
Life's just a joke, shared between me and you!

A Canvas of Aviary Visions

A parrot painted with colors bright,
Wore glasses so thick, what a funny sight!
It squawked a joke to a nearby crow,
'Why did the dove refuse to go?'

The crow just cawed and blinked its eye,
While the parrot laughed, 'To learn how to fly!'
They both burst out in raucous cheer,
In a showcase of feathers, it was clear!

An owl in a bow tie, still half asleep,
Said, 'I'm just here for the laughs, not the leap!'
It winked and dozed as others took flight,
Dreaming of puns that sparkled so bright.

A toucan strolled with a swagger so grand,
'These colors, my friends, are all unplanned!'
With laughter ringing, they filled the air,
In this world of whimsy, joy everywhere!

Altitude's Embrace

A balloon bird soared, no strings attached,
It giggled at clouds, feeling quite matched.
Said the sun to the moon, 'What have I missed?'
'You don't get it,' moon chuckled, 'This is bliss!'

A squirrel sneaked up in a gear so odd,
With goggles and scarf, it looked like a god!
It leaped from the tree, without any fear,
'Test flying's my job, so come cheers, my dear!'

An eagle squawked, 'Look at me, I'm suave!'
While trying to impress a lone, wandering dove.
But tripped on a twig, fell down with a yell,
'These heights sure are tough, can't you tell?'

So if ever you find your head in the air,
Remember the laughter sprinkled with care.
In a world up above, together we fly,
Making silly memories, you and I!

Shades of the Infinite Sky

A bluebird donned a cap, looking fine,
'This hat's for the party, and I'm feeling divine!'
It twirled on a branch, shaking a tail,
While friends gathered round, each telling a tale.

A robin jumped in on a wild little joke,
'Why don't we sing? It's a merry cloak!'
With a chirp and a tweet, they filled up the air,
Painting bright tunes, in camaraderie rare.

And as a hawk swooped by, unsure where to land,
It joined in the fun, just following the band.
They laughed till they cried, in the warm golden glow,
Under shades of the sky, with an avian show!

So next time you glance as the daylight departs,
Remember that laughter can dance in our hearts.
With every silly moment, our spirits will rise,
Creating our joy, under infinite skies!

Flutters of Infinity

A chicken dreamed of flying high,
It bucked and flapped, oh my, oh my!
The clouds just laughed, a feathery jest,
While birds around her pondered the quest.

She donned a hat, all cockamamie,
With goggles bright, she felt quite gamey.
On trampoline, she took her chance,
The local ducks went wild in a dance.

But gravity, that sneaky beast,
Said, 'Not today for the flying feast!'
With a thud and a wobble, back to the ground,
She learned that fun's where laughter is found.

Yet still she dreams of a giddy glide,
Wings made of dreams, it's all bona fide.
A life of whimsy, in sun and cheer,
The sky can wait, her laughter's here!

Ethereal Passages

A parrot read a book on flight,
With glasses perched, it looked so bright.
The words were silly, the pictures grand,
He plotted courses over land.

At sunset's glow, he took to air,
Flapping wildly, quite the scare!
But nettles poked his puzzled beak,
Landing softly in a peak.

An owl hooted, 'Oh, what flair!'
'You look more like a circus bear!'
They both dissolved in a feathered fit,
As dreams took flight, no need to quit.

A whimsical world of jokes and glee,
Each sunset was a comedy spree.
'Til one day he soared, lost in delight,
He found new friends, sharing the light!

The Spirit's Soft Embrace

In a forest where the giggles grow,
A wise old squirrel put on a show.
With acorns dancing, they played all day,
Inviting critters to join in the fray.

A dove flew by with a silly hat,
'Hey there, friends! Who's next for a splat?'
They all lined up, for a grand old dive,
To see who could make the best little jive.

A rabbit bounced, then fell with a thud,
'My puffy tail is now caked with mud!'
They laughed till they cried, oh what a treat!
In nature's embrace, they tapped their feet.

With spirit so soft, they joined as one,
Turning mischief into great fun.
A tapestry woven with giggles and grace,
In the heart of the woods, there's always a space!

Beyond the Limits of Possibility

A crow with a knack for cooking up pie,
Invited the critters, both low and high.
With sprinkles of mischief and a dash of jest,
They feasted like kings, the bugs smashed the rest.

A badger proclaimed, 'This is quite divine!',
As raccoons rapped, stealing the shine.
The laughter erupted in a wild cacophony,
Even a fox joined the wacky symphony.

They tried to fly, oh what a view,
With homemade wings, from popsicle glue.
They soared and crashed with giggles galore,
Past the clouds, as they landed once more.

With wings made of dreams and hearts that sing,
They discovered the joy that true fun can bring.
Together they found, in each clumsy spree,
The limits of laughter are wild and free!

The Dance of Skybound Remnants

The birds above, they twirl and spin,
In a game of tag, they always win.
With flapping wings and silly squawks,
They glide like clowns on aerial walks.

A crow tries to do a little jig,
But lands too hard, it looks quite big.
The sparrows giggle, they point and tease,
As he fluffs his feathers in the breeze.

Up high they laugh in cloud-filled glee,
While all the humans spill their tea.
A pigeon struts with an air so rare,
"Watch me dance," he shouts with flair!

When twilight comes, they bow and sway,
In feathered costumes, they'll steal the day.
With ruffled pride, they take a bow,
And scatter off to wonder how.

Echoes in the Wind

The whispers float on gentle air,
A little breeze that plays with hair.
A parakeet starts to sing a tune,
While kangaroos dance under the moon.

The sound of giggles, soft and neat,
As squirrels gather for a treat.
They toss around some acorn hats,
And laugh aloud, those silly bats!

On windy days, the echoes ring,
While all the weirdos dance and sing.
A chicken flaps, lost in delight,
"Hey, I can fly!"—what a funny sight!

The clouds above roll with a grin,
As nature joins this raucous din.
Together they burst, in colorful cheer,
With humor soaring, far and near.

A Tapestry of Soaring Souls

In the sky of winks and whimsical plays,
A raccoon dons a cape, striding in rays.
With a somersault, he steals the show,
"Who needs a stage? I'm the star, you know!"

The owls hoot laughing, their wisdom absurd,
As the sloth takes the stage, not saying a word.
"I'm flying high in the hearts of all,"
He mumbles with glee, then takes a small fall.

With twirls and twists, they twist divine,
A goat on a tightrope starts to shine.
As he leaps and bounds with over-the-top flair,
"Now that's just ridiculous!" gasps the bear.

When dusk paints colors, wild and bold,
The laughter warms, a treasure to hold.
In this tapestry woven with joyful souls,
They dance like confetti, unbound by their roles.

Celestial Veils at Dusk

At dusk, the sky dons a shimmering dress,
As giggles rustle, causing no stress.
A penguin slides on clouds with glee,
"Hey, look at me—I'm flying free!"

With moonbeams laughing, the stars join in,
As a bear juggles berries with a grin.
"Catch!" he yells, as they tumble and roll,
In a cosmic circus, that's their goal!

The crows play catch, with sticks that soar,
While crickets chirp jokes that leave them sore.
An owl flips pancakes on a moonlit fire,
"Don't forget syrup!" is his quip of desire.

As the night grows deep, the fun won't cease,
With laughter echoing, a sweet release.
These celestial antics, absurd yet bright,
Turn the dark canvas into pure delight!

Wings Unclipped by Time

A chicken in a top hat struts,
He dreams of flight and fancy cuts.
With wings so bright, they hardly sync,
He flaps and flops, then stops to think.

A pigeon in a cape, quite bold,
Saves sandwich crumbs, they'll never fold.
His sidekick, a sparrow with a grin,
Knows all the spots where crumbs begin.

A duck in shades, he takes a dive,
With rainbows splashing, oh what a jive!
He quacks a tune, a bizarre ballet,
While onlookers laugh, "What a day!"

While geese in scarves waddle and prance,
Creating punchlines with each funny glance.
In feathers and laughs, time flies away,
But who knew birds could play ballet?

Choreography of Clouds

The clouds have gathered, a fluffy crew,
They've got an audition, fancy and new.
With pirouettes and big balloon moves,
They bounce with laughter, no need for grooves.

A cumulus twirls in a polka dot dress,
While cirrus takes the stage, feeling quite blessed.
Thunderheads clapped, though often they grumble,
Each stomp a giggle, a whimsical rumble.

They puff and they puff, a joyful brigade,
Floating through skies where the sunshine played.
A smiling sun stops to catch the sight,
"Who knew clouds could dance with such delight?"

At sunset, they bow, in hues so bright,
While stars in the background cheer in the night.
Tomorrow they promise a rerun on high,
With feathers of laughter, oh me, oh my!

Celestial Wrappings of Dawn

The roosters crow, but in silly tones,
Instead of wake-up, they sing funny drones.
A ticket to laughter, the morning sings loud,
As jokes fly about, making frolic a crowd.

Sunrise giggles with colorful beams,
Wrapping the earth in whimsical dreams.
A squirrel dances with toast in its paws,
"Well, who ate my acorns?" it humorously claws.

Dewdrops tumble like laughter so bright,
Each drop a chuckle, in morning's first light.
While shadows skedaddle, a peculiar sight,
Mischief awakens with each fold of night.

The world gets a blanket of soft, silly hues,
With butterflies joining in colorful views.
As dawn unfolds, with joy in the air,
The day's our stage, with laughter to share.

Shimmering Skies Await

A butterfly flutters wearing a bow,
He's late to the dance, he's missing the show.
With the ants forming lines in a wild parade,
They giggle and trip, what a fine charade!

The dragonflies zoom in a whirlpool twirl,
Chasing sunbeams, as daisies unfurl.
"Let's catch some rays, and maybe a laugh!"
While ladybugs sketching their own epitaph.

The sun's a joker, he pokes and he prods,
Tickling the trees with playful little nods.
As comets streak by with a wink and a grin,
They shout, "Join the fun! Come on, jump in!"

A starlit end, and the laughter still plays,
While moonbeams shimmer in countless ways.
As day's curtain falls, so sweet and light,
With all of us chuckling till the next night!

Silken Threads of Air

In the breeze, a whisper flies,
A clumsy bird in goofy ties.
With a hop and a jig, it takes to the sky,
Chasing its dreams as the clouds pass by.

The sun shines bright on this feathered fool,
Who thought the sky was a swimming pool.
Flapping and floundering, it makes quite a splash,
As some frightened fish watch in a panicked dash.

It dances on currents, a hilarious sight,
Sprinkling laughter in morning light.
With a wobble and wiggle, it aims for a glide,
But tumbling mid-air is the funnier side.

So here's to the antics of those up above,
Who bring us delight with their clumsy love.
For when skies are clear and spirits are high,
We cheer for the birds who aim for the sky.

Celestial Quills

A duck with a dream to reach for the stars,
Wore a hat made of twigs and shiny cigars.
It quacked with ambition, "Catch me if you can!"
As it paddled in circles, a feathered old man.

Bella the pigeon, dressed up for a show,
With polka dots and stripes, all aglow.
She strutted around, quite proud of her flair,
Until she slipped on a banana and fell through the air.

A seagull sipping coffee at sunrise,
Laughs at the antics of pigeons that rise.
With a bagel in tow and a wink of an eye,
He flips off a rooftop like he's meant to fly.

So cheers to the chirps and giggles they spread,
As they dance through the skies with a laugh up ahead.
Their quills may be silly, but their joy is quite real,
Bringing smiles to our faces, that's their ideal.

The Dance of Winged Shadows

On the dance floor of clouds, shadows swayed,
Bouncing with laughter like kids at a parade.
With beaks for guitars and wings for a beat,
They jived to the rhythm of their silly feet.

A raven in shades tried to steal the show,
While a finch in a tutu goes twirling to and fro.
The owl's too cool, but loves a good pun,
While the sparrows, they chirp, "Let's have some fun!"

With every flap and a flurry of tail,
They form a conga line, a feathered trail.
The fun never halts, it's a riot up there,
As they drop their inhibitions without a care.

So if you find feathers upon the ground,
Know a party's been had; just listen for sound.
The dance of the shadows, they glide and they play,
Bringing joyous delight to brighten your day.

Skylight Serenade

A robin in a top hat sings songs of delight,
With a chirp and a hop, it takes to the height.
It invites all the critters to gather around,
For a concert in air, a melodious sound.

The stars keep their rhythm, twinkling in time,
As a woodpecker drops in with a bongo chime.
They groove in the moonlight, a whimsical night,
Where the owls in tuxedos applaud with delight.

Each note is a giggle, each chorus a cheer,
As the clouds play along with no hint of a fear.
The lyrics are silly, the melodies swirl,
In this jovial gathering, just wait for a whirl.

So if you glance upwards when skies start to sing,
You might just catch sight of the joy they all bring.
In the great open air where the laughter's embraced,
The skylight serenade leaves smiles interlaced.

The Lullaby of Wings

All the birds are having dreams,
Sipping coffee with moonbeams.
One has socks—oh, what a sight!
They dance together, taking flight.

In pajama pants, they fluff and preen,
Chasing clouds, they're quite a scene.
With giggles that echo through the night,
They flip and flop, oh, what a flight!

A chicken clucks a silly tune,
While a duck twirls under the moon.
Each flap a laugh, a joyous spread,
Waking dreams with wings outspread.

So if you hear the laughter soar,
Join their dance, don't just ignore!
For when the dawn begins to break,
The giggly flock will surely quake!

Secrets of the Upper Breeze

In the trees, gossip flies high,
Chickadees share secrets, oh my!
They chat about worms and fallen seeds,
While owls roll eyes and fulfill their needs.

An eagle's rumor took to wing,
Saying squirrels just can't sing.
But the squirrels hold a secret fair,
Twirling nuts with graceful flair!

The sparrows wear the latest trend,
Strutting 'round like they're the best friend.
While doves just coo and shake their heads,
At all these silly, feathered threads.

So gather 'round and lend an ear,
To all the chatter, loud and clear!
The breeze carries tales, fresh as mint,
And if you listen, you might just squint!

Light as Air

A parrot dressed in polka dots,
Claims it's light, though weighs a lot.
When asked to fly, it flutters low,
Then trips on branches, putting on a show.

A hummingbird sips on sweet delight,
But crashes into a bug—it's quite a sight!
With dizzy spins, it sways around,
"Oh, I meant to land, not hit the ground!"

A sparrow hops with flair and pride,
But often slips; it can't decide.
To fly or hop, oh what a fuss!
Then giggles break, they're all a plus.

So as they flit both near and far,
Remember, flight's a funky star!
Being light as air is true and real,
But laughter's weight is hard to conceal!

Soft as Thought

A robin ponders what to wear,
A hat, a bow, or none to spare?
With fluff and ruffles, soft and nice,
It chooses socks—oh, what a spice!

Invention blooms like petals bright,
As pigeons strut with all their might.
They fashion ties from bits of string,
Claiming fashion's the real thing!

While doves debate the latest trends,
The finches giggle, making amends.
"Wear your heart?" one squeaks with glee,
"Let's start a brand, just you and me!"

So take a note from birdie lore,
And wear what makes you want to soar!
For soft as thought, as laughter too,
Is what makes a feathered friendship true!

The Feathered Edge of Day

At the dawn, with coffee brewed,
Birds awaken, in a cheerful mood.
With sleepy songs, they start to chirp,
An alarm clock? Nay! It's just a burp!

As sunlight paints a golden hue,
A rooster crows, "Oh, what's to do?"
While sparrows twirl, stealing the show,
They rattle on with silly glow!

A crow in shades of midnight black,
Claims it knows all—a real wise crack.
But as it caws, it spills some beans,
On neighbor's lost, unused machines!

So join the fun, as sunlight wakes,
With laughter echoing through the lakes.
For on the edge of every day,
Is joy amid the comical fray!

Secrets of the Celestial Expanse

A shout from the stars, or is it a joke?
The cosmos is laughing, wrapped in a cloak.
Planets are tumbling in a giggling spree,
While comets play tag, oh what sights to see!

A moon wearing glasses, just peeking through dust,
Claims it can dance, but it's lost all its rust.
Jupiter just told a pun so absurd,
Even Saturn's rings spun, it simply concurred!

Aliens sneaking on a light-speed chase,
Waving their antennas, oh what a face!
They've got their own jokes, too silly to share,
And meteors blushing like they're caught in a dare!

Each star holds a secret, a laugh and a wink,
Cosmic giggles observed, more fun than you think.
So join in the jest, let your worries unwind,
In the expanse of the sky—a joy you will find!

Swaying with the Skybound Spirits

Clouds are like dancers, swaying so free,
They leap and they twirl, from the mountains to sea.
With a tickle of breeze, they puff up with glee,
Making shapes of delight, like a fluffy marquee!

Those spirits are cheeky, they swirl and they whip,
They hide from the sun, then do a quick flip.
Winking at rainbows, playing peek-a-boo,
While sunlight bursts forth to join in the crew!

Mist joins the party, it drapes like a veil,
Each droplet a dancer, with their own little tale.
Giggles arise from a warm summer night,
As stars join the mosh pit and dance with delight!

So let your toes tap, feel the joy of the air,
Swaying with spirits, without a single care.
For laughter erupts in the wide-open sky,
As clouds swirl around—oh, hear their soft sigh!

A Canvas of Cloudbound Whispers

Overhead, the clouds are a painter's delight,
Sketching out jokes in the soft morning light.
Each swirl is a chuckle, each puffy design,
A canvas of giggles, oh how they'll entwine!

The sun drips with humor, a golden prankster,
Casting shadows that dance, a jolly jester.
With each passing breeze, another laugh flies,
The sky's endless palette, a feast for our eyes!

Puffy sheep racing, in a heavenly race,
Tiptoeing quietly, they vanish without trace.
And the stars whisper secrets when night starts to creep,
In a twinkling duet, making the cosmos leap!

So lift up your gaze to that whimsical spread,
Where laughter and colors fill dreams in your head.
A canvas above, where the giggles collide,
Every sigh on the wind—a joy you can't hide!

Horizon's Embrace

At the edge of the world, where giggles collide,
The sun starts to yawn, with a cheeky glide.
Its rays, like tickles, play hide and seek,
While shadows jump out, oh, what a peek!

The ocean chuckles, as waves tickle shore,
Gathers the laughter that's been there before.
Horizon's a prankster, pulling up the mist,
With a wink and a smile, it can't be dismissed!

Clouds gather for gossip, trading old tales,
Of raindrops and sunshine, the game never fails.
Like a band of jesters, they burst into cheer,
While the mountains hum softly, drawing us near!

So come take a stroll down this funny old path,
Where every horizon is bursting with laughs.
In the hugs of the twilight, you'll find sweet embrace,
In the giggles of dusk, you'll discover your place!

Carried on the Breath of Angels

A pigeon cooed with all its might,
Twisting through the sky so bright,
It missed the ledge, gave quite a shout,
And landed on a cat, no doubt.

She thought she'd soar like she was queen,
Instead, she took a seat, unseen,
On fluffy clouds, she took a ride,
With squirrels laughing by her side.

Unseen by folks with eyes on ground,
They see her bobbing all around,
With wings all flapping, out of sync,
She clucks and giggles, what a wink!

The wind, it teased her playful hair,
The clouds, they swung her everywhere,
She tried to flap to make a point,
But ended up just bending joints.

The Art of Flying Free

There once was a bird, plump and round,
Who fancied he was joy unbound,
He leapt from heights that made folks yell,
Not realizing he'd do swell.

With one small flap, he hit the breeze,
But flew straight into prickly trees,
He shook his head and grumbled too,
While birds cawed laughter right on cue.

His fellow fliers had their sleek grace,
But he just wished to join the race,
With a bit of charm, no skill at all,
He flapped his wings, but took a fall.

Those tiny flocks would soar and glide,
While he just flopped or slipped and sighed,
Yet he would puff his mighty chest,
And hope that next time he'd fly best.

Dreamscapes on the Wind

In a land where dreams are spun with glee,
Clouds were pillows, wild and free,
A cow took flight, oh what a sight,
With polka dots and pure delight!

She wobbled high, quite unsure,
Stirring up giggles, pure and pure,
"Just a hop!" she said, all in a twirl,
"Next lap around, I'll give it a whirl!"

Kites danced on threads of silly fate,
A grand parade for skies to create,
The cow mooed tunes that gleefully rang,
As bunnies joined in, all slapstick sang.

With each fluffy leap, laughter arose,
To twirl through the day in perfect prose,
Each mishap crafted in light of whim,
While the stars giggled in evenings dim.

The Pulse of the Atmosphere

The breeze chuckled, whispering low,
As clouds fumbled in a dance, a show,
A squirrel donned a tiny hat,
And pranced around, all shiny and fat!

He zipped and zoomed, a true delight,
With every twirl, he took to flight,
But tangled up in string so tight,
He juggled air while in mid-flight.

Around the trees, out absolutely,
He zoomed past friends who squealed with glee,
They joined the fun, made motions bold,
A circus act worth more than gold!

They danced on winds, both giddy and free,
Creating a ruckus for all to see,
With laughter echoing far and near,
In the grand pulse of skies, oh dear!

www.ingramcontent.com/pod-product-compliance
Lightning Source LLC
Chambersburg PA
CBHW070321120526
44590CB00017B/2774